HERCULES FLEXED

Tales of the Mighty Greg Fischer

By Ela Hodosky, A.S., B.A., M.S. Ed., M.S. S.B.L., S.D.L

HERCULES FLEXED

Tales of the Mighty Greg Fischer

Ela Hodosky A.S., B.A., M.S. Ed., M.S. S.B.L., S.D.L

Published in the United States of America

First Edition 2018

Grateful acknowledgement is made to the Suffolk County Democratic CD-1 candidates, all photographs were taken at public events.

Hodosky, Pamela

HERCULES FLEXED

Tales of the Mighty Greg Fischer

Designed by Pamela Hodosky.

Photography by Pamela Hodosky.

For Greg, The Visionary Candidate, with Love.

pol·i·ti·cian ˌpälə'tiSHən
noun

> **politician**; plural noun: **politicians**
> a person who is professionally involved in
> politics, especially as a holder of or a
> candidate for an elected office.
>
> > *Syn.* legislator, elected official,
> > statesman, stateswoman, public
> > servant;
> > senator, congressman,
> > congresswoman;
> > *informal* politico, pol
> > "campaigning politicians make
> > more promises than they can
> > keep"

U.S: a person who acts in a manipulative and devious
way, typically to gain advancement within an
organization.

Contents

HERCULES FLEXED

Tales of the Mighty Greg Fischer
Vol. 1

1. <u>Meet the Candidate:</u>

<u>Gregory-John Fischer</u>

<u>Vote for a Turnaround.</u>

Campaign 2018 began with the County of

Suffolk attracting nationwide attention due to

the heavy gang activity related to the notorious

El Salvadorian gang known as MS-13.

The first candidates in the campaign line-up are

vying for the Congressional District 1 (CD-1), a

seat held by a Republican. Greg Fischer is the NY

State Senate district 1 (SD-1) Democratic

candidate. Greg was born in New York City and

moved to Calverton in the wake of the 9-11

attack, where he was a volunteer responder. He graduated with three business degrees: General Management (CUNY), Finance (SUNY at New Paltz,) and Operations Management (SUNY at Albany.) He is a single Father of 4, with two children being educated in the Riverhead Central School District. As a private citizen, for the past 12 years, Greg has injected himself into local politics in an effort to change the destructive path of Suffolk County politics which was rocked the previous year, by scandals that imprisoned the Chief of Police and indicted the District Attorney who held an elected position.

The county teeters on bankruptcy and was made lawless by dirty cops, deemed by the incarcerated Chief to be "the palace guard," who had no oversight, and a crooked court system where Judges are elected by a pay to play system; conditions that promoted MS-13 gang activity as a way of survival. The 2018 Congressional race (Congressional District 1 – "CD-1") campaign kicks off the campaign season that will proceed onward towards the 2018 Senate campaign; in Senate District 1 (SD-1) Greg Fischer intends to win. My understanding of the intricacies of Suffolk County politics come from my 30 year run as a politicians wife, community activist and Photographer. I am a lifelong resident of Suffolk County. Greg Fischer invited me to shadow him as he began his 2018 campaign, allowing me unlimited access to his professional and political life. His personal and family life became evident to me as I monitored his daily activities. I was always treated with respect and whenever I engaged his family and loved ones, I was welcomed. The photographs chronicle the campaign trail as it begins with the Congressional candidate race and advances to the Senate race. Eventually, I became his

Campaign Manager. The Congressional primary

that will determine the Democratic

Congressional

candidate has just

occurred.

The Senate race has not yet begun. Retired

business executive, Single Father, Greg Fischer

spends his limited free time attending

community functions that will enable him to

make the connections he will need to raise

funds and meet constituents who can volunteer

for his campaign. There are usually events

happening every single day. Greg, as a single

Dad, tries to attend at least one event during

the week, on the single evening he doesn't have

his kids and then one on each weekend day that

he doesn't have his kids. His family and children

support his continuing efforts to bring a

turnaround to his community and county even

though it takes many hours away from his

family.

March 2018

The Southold
Housing Crisis
Seminar, East
Marion, New York.

Greg Fischer
speaking

With Dr. Rona
Smith.

There is no guidebook. The

campaign begins at the grassroots level, talking

to the people in the streets and at community

events. There are no assigned mentors in this

group, no school of campaigning, each candidate learns the hard way and small mistakes exact large punishments. Greg is the senior candidate and he has been involved for 12 years and many of the younger candidates come to him for advice. He helps every candidate without prejudice. Candidates usually attend Democratic Party committee meetings, become interested in the issues concerning the community and begin to determine how they want to participate. Meeting attendance, volunteering and fund raising for donations are the incubators for future candidates. Some are

Political Science majors in college, many are the

children of Politicians.   I accompany Greg to

many of these events, chronicling the people

and places through photographs taken on the

spur of the moment, as they approach Greg. I

always ask for the picture, as Greg speaks

privately with the individual, guiding, offering

advice and encouragement, sometimes arguing.

Politics is a dirty game for a clean candidate.

March 2018, (L to R,) Attorney Bill Ian Jurow, Mastic, NY
Ela Hodosky, Campaign Manager for Greg Fischer, and
Greg Fischer at the Independent Party Social Club
meeting, Islip- MacArthur Airport, Ronkonkoma, New
York.

2. *The Economics of Power.*

The Battle of Life

In the battle of life it is not the critic who counts;
Not the man who points out how the strong man
stumbled, or where the doer of a deed could have
done better. The credit belongs to the man who is
actually in the arena; whose face is marred by dust
& sweat & blood; who strives valiantly; who errs
and comes short again and again because there is no
effort without error and shortcoming; who does
actually strive to do the deeds; who knows the great
enthusiasms, the great devotion, spends himself in a
worthy cause; who at best knows in the end the
triumph of high achievement; and at worst if he
fails, at least fails while daring greatly, so that his
place shall never be with those cold and timid souls
who have tasted neither victory nor defeat.

       -Theodore Roosevelt (R)

The candidates stepped into the 2018 race on the heels of a scandal that rocked the Suffolk County Police Department as the Chief of the department, was sentenced to jail in 2016. In the course of his demise it was revealed that the Chief had suffered an auto "accident," staged upon him by the lead investigator of corruption for the Office of the Suffolk County District Attorney. The District Attorney had supported him for the Chief position in 2011, he considered him to be a friend. The Chief knows the fraud ring operating the staged auto accidents,

because he helped to crack it with the

assistance of the Suffolk County District

Attorney in 2003. The New York Times

reported the details, *"Investigators Say

Fraud Ring Staged Thousands of Crashes,"*

by Patrick Healy, August 13, 2003. The

chief knows there is no hope for him, the

2003 investigation resulted in 567

indictments of doctors, psychiatrists,

chiropractors, dentists all involved in a

Scheme to Defraud yet only 28

indictments were made public. Powerful

people with a tremendous combined financial base which grew stronger when Andrew M. Cuomo garnered 63% of the vote and left his job as New York State Attorney General to become the Governor of New York. Ties to Russia are clear as indicated by the many Russian immigrants involved in the staged auto accident ring dubbed "Operation Boris." Now, this evil economic engine was about to crush him and 91 year old Suffolk County Supreme Court Judge, Leonard D. Wexler sentenced the Chief to 46 months in jail. By 2018, Wexler has died, the

District Attorney and his lead investigator

of corruption are indicted and our

candidates need the courage to step into

the political ring to try to make things

right again. It's almost impossible, it's like

watching Hercules, Greg Fischer has

battled political corruption for 12 years.

In 2011, Governor Andrew M. Cuomo and

the New York State Legislature

consolidated the New York State

Insurance Department and the New York

State Banking Department and created

the New York state Department of

Financial Services, destroying any hope of

halting the increasing wave of staged

auto accidents being inflicted upon the

residents of Suffolk County. Now, Suffolk

County, New York has the highest

number of auto accidents in the entire

country. Under the state's no-fault

insurance laws, anyone injured in a car

accident can receive up to $50,000 for

medical care. That means the doctors,

psychiatrists, chiropractors and dentists

are going to profit again. The law also

enables insurance investigators to surveil,

by Private Investigators (who are often

off duty and retired Police officers, who

are also Volunteer Firemen) anyone

involved in the auto accident, especially

those experiencing home foreclosure.

Suffolk County has the highest number of

military Veterans in the entire state of

New York, they are the volunteer

firemen, and Suffolk County, New York

has the highest number of pending

foreclosures in the entire country. With

good reason, the general public perceives

ALL politicians as criminals. Suffolk

County is the second most corrupt county

in the nation, with a strong "Deep State"

base. Femicide rates are incalculable and

only 19% of the population votes. The

candidates know this 19% consists largely

of Senior citizens, Veterans, Teacher

Unions and Police Unions. The random

voter is rare. The young voter is even

more rare. It's a dicey environment,

controlled largely by the Suffolk County

Board of Elections. Located just across

the street from Suffolk County Police

headquarters, the SC Board of Elections

collects voter registrations via individual

applications handed out in the local high

schools and through the New York State

Department of Motor Vehicles when

applicants submit their date of birth and

Social Security number to receive a

driver's license. The Voter Registration

forms are broken, when improperly

folded, they never reach the voter. Many

private citizens complain to Greg Fischer

as he campaigns for State Senate, a seat

held by a 42 year corrupt incumbent.

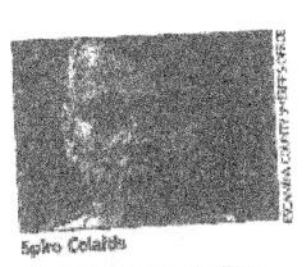

MAN CHARGED WITH VOTING TWICE IN 2016

BY RACHEL UDA
rachel.uda@newsday.com

A Manhasset man is being charged with voting twice in the 2016 presidential election.

Spiro Colaitis, 57, voted at the polls in Nassau County on Election Day, and by mail-in ballot in Escambia County in Florida, according to the Office of the State Attorney in Pensacola, Florida.

Colaitis turned himself in to the Escambia County Sheriff's Office on Thursday and was charged with casting more than one ballot in an election, a felony, according to the state attorney's office. He was released the same day on $2,500 bail, online arrest records show.

Colaitis, who is the assistant superintendent for district operations for the Malverne school district, did not respond to a request for comment.

The school district declined to comment, calling it "a personal matter and currently under law enforcement review."

An investigation by the state attorney's office found that Colaitis has not lived in Pensacola since 2005 and sold his property there before 2010, according to an affidavit filed with an arrest report.

The Nassau district attorney's office will look into the case, said spokeswoman Miriam Sholder. "This is a Florida prosecution and as such, we are unfamiliar with the charges," Sholder said. "We will speak to Florida authorities about the matter."

Colaitis also served as commander of the New York Naval Militia. He has taken a leave of absence from the role effective Tuesday, a spokesman for the state Division of Military and Naval Affairs said.

He is scheduled to be arraigned April 26, the Florida State Attorney's Office said.

Where there's smoke there's fire.

Once licensed to drive by the New York

State Department of Motor Vehicles the

driver needs auto insurance; a

Comprehensive **L**oss **U**nderwriting

Exchange report is created to enable

insurance and real estate agents to rate

insurance policies for auto and home. It is

referred to as a "C.L.U.E." report. The

CLUE report is a dossier of every single

American driver and is created and

controlled by LexisNexis located, locally,

in Melville, New York, next to the only

daily newspaper for Suffolk and Nassau

Counties; "Newsday." LexisNexis is also

located just across the street from the

Regional office of the Federal Bureau of

Investigation (FBI.) In the middle of this

cluster, providing power to everyone is

the largest L.I.P.S.E.G office in Suffolk

County. In 2013, New York Governor

Cuomo signed into law a bill to privatize

the Long Island Power Authority creating

L.I PSEG which inherited a $7 Billion dollar

debt and requires customers who require

electric service to present their New York

State Driver's License and provide their

Social Security number, especially the

single Mother.

Dragging LIPA to court

BY MARK HARRINGTON
mark.harrington@newsday.com

- Divorced mother of 5 seeks $700,000 in dispute
- Case stems from $7G in arrears by then-husband

Emma Gunter is acting as her own lawyer in an eight-year battle.

All Emma Gunter wanted, she says, was electric service to her Rockville Centre home and a LIPA account in her own name.

After being jailed, temporarily losing custody of her children and suffering damage to her former home — most stemming, she alleges, from her attempts to keep the power on with her own Long Island Power Authority account — Gunter will get her day in federal court tomorrow.

There, she is seeking more than $700,000 in reparations for her three-year dispute with the utility and social services a decade ago.

The crux of the case is Gunter's claim that LIPA, then operated by KeySpan and National Grid, unlawfully declined to establish an account in her name because the house she was taking over in a divorce had $7,000 in arrears under her husband's name. A filing on Thursday lists 27 separate instances in which she charges the authority violated its own rules.

"They simply exhorted me to pay my ex-husband's bill," charged Gunter, 54, a mother of five who spent 20 years in the airline industry.

LIPA, in court papers, claims Gunter failed at first to provide the needed document to establish an account, and that it ultimately did so in her name once she did. Representatives for LIPA and National Grid declined to comment.

Gunter's eight-year effort to bring the case to trial is an unlikely tale. She is acting as her own attorney while LIPA for a decade has used the law firm Cullen and Dykman to argue its case. Judges have rejected LIPA's efforts to dismiss the suit.

"I think it's quite rare that people find a way to federal court and get through the process," particularly without a lawyer, said Gerald Norlander, past executive director of the Public Utility Law Project, which defends ratepayers in efforts to restore utilities. Less usual, he said, is that utilities seek to recover arrears associated with a home, when service turns over to a new account holder.

Gunter said she was living in Minneapolis and working for Northwest Airlines in 2006 when her high-school age son called saying his father, whom Gunter was divorcing, was "unresponsive." She returned to Long Island to live with her children and began proceedings to buy the Rockville Centre house after her husband moved out.

What he left, she said, was a $7,000 LIPA bill in his name tied to the house. It wasn't long before LIPA came to collect.

Power "was on for one day, the next day it was off," she said. "I called and said, 'I need to transfer the account to my name.' I took them a deposit. They said, 'You can't have an account, your husband has an account, you need to pay his arrears.'"

LIPA in court papers says it "never required her to pay" her ex-husband's bill. Nevertheless, LIPA said, "since she admitted that she owned" the home since mid-2006, electric service to the home "would have benefited her, and she should have been responsible for the service from the date she took ownership."

Norlander disagreed. "They cannot deny service to any person unless that person owes money for an account in his or her name for prior service," he said, citing state law and a precedent-setting case he won for PULP.

LIPA in court papers also claims Gunter "never supplied LIPA with a copy of the deed at that time" and that its "business records do not show [Gunter] ever applied for service" from 2006 through the first eight months of 2008. She denies the claims. Gunter said she made three separate tariff-permitted verbal applications, and never received written notice of rejection, as is required.

"LIPA's tariff doesn't specify a deed as the only proof required for service. The tariff requires only "reasonable proof" that the applicant became responsible for service to a home, proof that "may" include a deed, "bill of sale, etc." Gunter said she brought closing papers, but didn't have the deed until end of 2006. When she supplied it, she charged, LIPA still demanded she pay her ex-husband's bill.

LIPA, in court papers, acknowledged shutting off power to the house at least three times. Gunter said she paid more than $4,500 of her husband's arrears. But the spotty electrical service eventually caught the attention of Nassau County Social Services.

According to media accounts from October 2008, a social worker sent to Gunter's home "as part of an ongoing court case" found the house had "no heat or running water, and electricity was being provided by a generator in the backyard." Gunter said the house had water, but the heat was electric.

Federal court papers filed against Gunter by Nassau Social Services point to a state action that "clearly accused Emma Gunter of failing to have a utility account and thus endangering the welfare of children who resided in the home."

Gunter was arrested on charges of child endangerment, obstructing government administration and criminal contempt after refusing to disclose the whereabouts of two of her children and grandchildren.

The following year, she spent four months in Nassau County jail on the contempt charges, she said. LIPA said it established electricity to the home in her name in November 2008, "after supplying a copy of her deed."

Gunter, who is of African-American and Cherokee Indian descent, said service in her name came more than two years too late. In court papers she charges she was the subject of discrimination based on race and gender. She also believes she is not alone.

"If you come from a house with arrears, you don't get the same treatment as a house without arrears," she said. "A house doesn't have arrears, a person has arrears. They can't extort people for money under the threat of excluding them from service."

Seeing constant and chronic injustice, Greg Fischer brings suit upon the utility company.

The candidates, Americans all, step up with hopes of enabling the democracy that supports our American freedoms. They put their lives on the line, they offer up their children and families and safety. They know they are on the front line of democracy with small weapons and many silent supporters who like children, depend on them to keep on fighting for the 242 year old democracy known as the United States of America. In 2011, when the New York State Governor created the New York State

Department of Financial Services, the American,

Gregory John Fischer an Economist, who like

thousands of other Suffolk County homeowners

is being crushed by taxes, traffic and the high

cost of living in corrupt Suffolk County, as an

Economist, realizes the precarious state of

Suffolk County and has already announced; "I'm

going to run once a year forever!"

May 2018, NYS Attorney General Eric

Schneiderman, resigned amidst a sex scandal.

April 2018, Governor, Andrew M. Cuomo (a former
New York State Attorney General) at the New York
Democrat Rally, Holtsville, Long Island, New York, on
the stage with Rich Schaffer, Suffolk County
Democratic Party Chairman. Cuomo appointed newly
elected Eric Schneiderman as Attorney General in '11.

With Congressional candidate Elaine DiMasi (r) at the
New York Democrats rally, Holtsville, NY.

3. ***<u>The Visionary Candidate.</u>***

FRONT   BACK

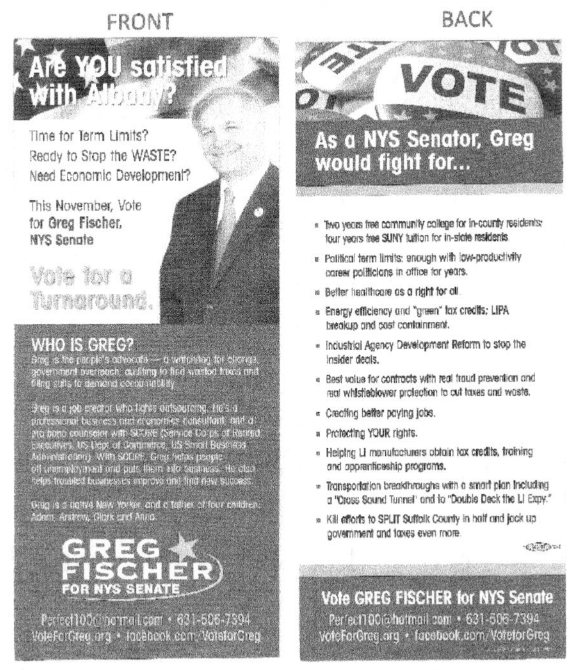

The campaign literature called "the Palm Card," all the candidates have them to handout as they circulate among crowds at events, never knowing who they will encounter. It contains pertinent information related to the candidates' platform, and issues that are important to the candidate. The Greg Fischer for NYS Senate card is three years old, undated, it never changes. Greg understands that he has a great chance of losing the election, he has them printed in bulk, never changing his message.

His desire to build a "Cross Sound

Tunnel," and to "Double Deck the Long

Island Expressway," astound many short

sighted Long Islanders who fail to see the

benefits including the fact that the tunnel

will pay for itself in tolls. Also failing to

see the need for job creation,

Congressman Lee Zeldin tells Greg,

Above, May 6, 2018, With Congressman Lee Zeldin, Riverhead VFW Post 2476, Pancake Breakfast.

"It was a good idea…40 years ago." Economist

Greg states, "We need it."

Congressman Zeldin responded by asking Greg

Fischer, "Are you still registered as a

Democrat?"

Above, May 6, 2018, With Conservative, Charles Clampett at the VFW Post 2476, Pancake Breakfast.

Jobs, jobs and more jobs, visionary infrastructure projects to move Long Island forward are critical to the message of the Greg

Fischer for Senate campaign, even housing issues can't be solved without jobs.

L to R: April 2018, Atty, Blaire Fellows, Dale Javino, Greg Fischer, Bill Jurow, Center Moriches, New York.

4. *West towards Brookhaven, NY.*

Senate District 1 lies mainly in the 5 Eastern

Long Island towns which include Riverhead,

Southampton, Southold, Peconic and

Greenport. A small portion of Senate District -1

(SD-1) lies in the Town of Brookhaven. The

Town of Brookhaven is a Republican stronghold,

which is supported by a strong union population

anchored by Brookhaven Memorial Hospital

Medical Center (BMHMC,) and Brookhaven

Laboratory, a former Army base. The Patchogue

and Bellport Fire Departments feed the hospital

via ambulance departments at the scene of

auto accidents occurring in the SCPD, 5th

precinct sector. Patchogue and Bellport Fire

Departments are the only fire departments in

Suffolk County with surplus budgets ($80 million

dollars.) Oyster Bay is the only fire department

in Nassau County with a surplus budget (see

"The Oyster Bay Way.") Dean Murray (R,)

Assemblyman, represents the 3rd Assembly

District. His local office is located in the North

Ocean Avenue Complex, North Ocean Avenue,

Patchogue, previously this complex housed the

offices for the Town of Brookhaven. The North

Ocean Avenue complex is managed by Realtor

James Roberts; next to the local Liberty Mutual Insurance office and a Zwanger Pesiri Radiology office, a Catholic Charities office and the local BOCES 2 office (which offers free mental health counseling for Teachers.) Eastern Suffolk Board of Cooperative Education Services interfaces with the New York State Department to review and issue licensing which include New York State Teacher certifications for public school teachers, Heating Ventilation and Air Conditioning (HVAC) licenses, Realtor licenses and Building Contractor licensing as well as Insurance licensing (auto home and life,)

Nursing licenses and Medical insurance billing and coding certifications (which are *international* codes which enable BMHMC to utilize the "Nighthawk network" in India to evaluate medical procedures performed on Americans in the United States,) as well as many others that require the oversight of the New York Department of State. BOCES, Bellport is located across the highway from BMHMC, and supplies the hospital with many, many employees from all the certification and licensing areas. Level 3 Communications, a Communication Consultant company is located just across the highway from ESBOCES. The <u>NSA</u> was accused of wiretapping large parts of data on the German <u>Internet Exchange Point</u> <u>DE-CIX</u> which was denied by Level 3, with headquarters in Berlin, and a few months later, the NSA was accused of tapping connections between Google and Yahoo data centers, in July 2013. In 2018, New York is listed last (#50,) on the list of the least free states in America.

November 1, 2017 (11117) Level 3, Bellport, New York, became CenturyLink.

A major contributor to the Dean Murray for Assembly campaign was Liberty Mutual

Insurance, Dean Murray owns the local Liberty Mutual Insurance office.

Dowling College, Oakdale, New York offers its Alumni low cost auto insurance through Liberty Mutual Insurance. Liberty Mutual Insurance offers an additional, free rider to the auto insurance policy offering a life insurance policy that can pay the spouse of a policy holder $1 million dollars if the insured commits suicide due to injuries sustained in an auto accident. An ex-spouse can also be a beneficiary.

Liberty Mutual Insurance has an office in Liverpool, New York also referred to as North

Syracuse for processing claims made on the

Dowling College Alumni policy,

North Syracuse, New York has an international

airport and a baseball stadium.

Dowling College President Robert. Gaffney

(previous Suffolk County Executive,) did create

the Dowling College Alumni Association Liberty

Mutual Insurance policy offer. Frank Mitchell

Corso Jr. is President of the Dowling College

Alumni Association. Connie Corso was Levy

appointed Budget Director. Once the ex-spouse

becomes a beneficiary, the million dollar rider

becomes a lifelong bounty on the head of the insured, even *after* the policy has expired.

Frank Mitchell Corso Jr. has familial ties to the Mitchell Cadillac dealership, which became J.D. Posillico Auto Dealership. Joseph Posillico sits on the Board of Directors at Dowling College alongside Matthew Cordero who also sits on the board of LIPSEG. For the poor, the New York State Office of Temporary Disability administers payments to delinquent or overdue PSEGLI accounts through the Home Energy Assistance Program - HEAP. In the Offices of the Town of Brookhaven, missing even a single months' payment of a residential PSEGLI bill

automatically triggers computer generated

foreclosure documents through the Suffolk

County Supreme Court. This trips another notice

to the Town of Brookhaven Code Enforcement

Department who begin to monitor garbage

pickups as they appear and more importantly

do not appear on the curb. Any garbage placed

at the curb can be searched by local authorities

to inspect for drug paraphernalia to engage law

enforcement who are also volunteers at the

local Fire Department. The Department of Social

Services can schedule an Adult Protective

Services and or a Child Protective Services visit,
always placed by an "anonymous, concerned
individual," which allows a Town, or County
Social Worker to do a clandestine "walk
through" the premises to ensure for "safety,"
but look for signs of drug use or signs of the
owner, occupant or tenant, packing up to leave.

Posillico construction, Mastic, New York holds
all Suffolk County contracts for LIPSEG line
maintenance. Posillico received county
contracts from Suffolk County Executive Steve
Levy. Mark Smith was his Deputy Director of
Communications, Jeff Szabo was his Deputy

County Executive. Connie Corso was appointed

Budget Director in 2007 by County Executive

Steve Levy. Attorney Maria "Mea" Knapp was

assigned to housing. Levy also hired Ex LIPA Vice

President (PSEGLI predecessor,) Ed Dumas,

Communications Director turned Chief Deputy

County Executive for Policy and

Communications. County Executive Steve Levy

appointed Jerry Gargiulo to the Suffolk County

Supreme Court, his son Joe Gargiulo works in

the Liberty Mutual Auto Insurance office that

processes the Dowling College Alumni

Association policies his co-worker is Eileen

Knapp, Dowling College Alumni Association

Liberty Mutual Liasion who is the daughter of

Levy housing administrator Maria (Mea) Knapp.

The family built the Knapp Cardiac Center

Building at Brookhaven Memorial Hospital

Medical Center, East Patchogue, New York in

2017, serviced by the Patchogue and Bellport

Fire departments and ambulance companies.

Under New York State No-fault insurance laws,

every motor vehicle accident provides $50,000

for injury related medical coverage. $50,000 for

each auto accident. Suffolk County, New York

has the highest number of auto accidents in the entire country.

New York State No-fault auto insurance allows motorists with open auto accidents to be surveilled by insurance investigators under the premise of verifying the injuries claimed in the accident to be valid and true. The Department of Motor Vehicle office located at 2799 NY-112, Medford, is in the 5th precinct.

Justice died in Suffolk County, New York on June 14, 2015 (Flag Day,) when retired officers Max Velasquez and Michael Schuierer were killed in simultaneous auto accidents. Suffolk County has the highest number of auto accidents in the entire country. Both officers died in auto "accidents," both occurred in the SC 5th Precinct.

Suffolk County has the highest number of foreclosures in the entire country.

On June 14, 2018 the Suffolk County District Attorney lost oversight of Asset Forfeiture funds when Legislator Rob Calarco proposed and passed a bill allowing oversight to go to the Suffolk County Legislature.

In 2010, Brookhaven Memorial Hospital, 101 Hospital Road, East Patchogue, New York, the last independently owned hospital on Long

Island, was ordered to pay a 2.5 million dollar

fine for Medicaid and Medicare fraud. In 2018

the hospital changed its name to Long Island

Medical Center, then changed it again a few

months later to Long Island Community

Hospital.

the dirt to plant flowers with girls from ·
hand was Suffolk County police commissioner Geraldine Hart, as they participated in th
Nursery in Holtsville donated the flowers for the beautification project.

Becoming Long Island Community Hospital

BY NICOLE ALLEGREZZA

Formerly known as Brookhaven Memorial Hospital Medical Center with a brief trial period as Long Island Medical Center, the only independent hospital left on Long Island has announced its official name change to Long Island Community Hospital — emphasizing community — during their annual employee barbecue last week.

Cynthia Ruf, vice president of branding and stakeholder relations, said the hospital plans to ease the transition by going by both names, BMHMC and LI Community Hospital, slowly making changes to things as small as business cards to as big as advertisements as needed.

"It has always been important to me to get this right. Now I can say, without hesitation, this name represents who we are ... everything we do is for the community. If I had to pick out one element of who makes me so proud of this organization, it is the connections our team make with our patients and guests every single day," said president and CEO Richard Margulis.

The new name was revealed during the annual employee barbecue in an effort to let the employees "own it" first. It came with a confetti pop and curtain drop reveal while taking an employee photo and was followed by a new rendition of the go cart karaoke video.

"We wanted the employees to know first, because it's really about them and the community they serve," said Ruf. "It's still the same concept behind the name 100 percent."

See LI COMMUNITY HOSPITAL on page 2

THE LONG ISLAND ADVANCE
JUNE 21, 2018

WEEKLY PERIODICAL

Suffolk County has a well known MS-13 gang problem. (Left) At Medford Department of Motor Vehicles, Line 13, Ticket R666. A Driver Abstract costs $10.00. It lists all accidents and tickets on a driving record. An insurance card is required to register a car. The insurance card is produced by an insurance agent after payment for a policy. The payment is determined by an agent after viewing the CLUE Report produced by LexisNexis. The CLUE Report is a dossier of every American driver, available to all law enforcement, and insurance agents,

Meanwhile, New York State Senate

District 1 Candidate, Greg Fischer

continues his 12 year march to restore

Democracy to Suffolk County as Suffolk

County Democrats choose Perry Gershon

to be their Congressional candidate in the

November 2018 election. Greg Fischer

becomes the New York State Democratic

Party State Senate Candidate from Senate

District 1.

Gershon hails turnout

Grechen Shirley challenges King to five debates

BY DAVID M. SCHWARTZ
david.schwartz@newsday.com

A surge in Democratic voters pushed Perry Gershon to his party's nomination on Tuesday, stoking hopes among Democrats for November, while Liuba Grechen Shirley deals a blow to the Suffolk political establishment.

Nearly twice as many voters turned out for the five-way 1st Congressional District primary compared to 2016, and East Hampton businessman Gershon took 36 percent of the vote. His next closest challenger, former Suffolk Legis. Kate Browning, took 18 percent. Gershon will face two-term Rep. Lee Zeldin (R-Shirley).

Out of 144,470 eligible voters, 20,193 voters turned out on Tuesday — 14.0 percent of voters, according to unofficial Suffolk board of elections returns. In the 1st District primary in 2016, 20,163 out of 115,654 voters turned out, or 7.5 percent. The figures don't include absentee voters for either year because

Perry Gershon

See how Long Islanders voted in this primary, district by district.
newsday.com/data